A Community Secret

For the Filipina
in an
Abusive Relationship

By Jacqueline R. Agtuca
in collaboration with the
Asian Women's Shelter

SEAL PRESS

The people appearing in photographs are in no way related to the people featured in this book. They appear for illustrative purposes only.

Cover photograph by Susan Breall
Book design by Diane Tani
The artwork, "Thoughts" (p. 36) and "Penance," (p. 45) is by Terry Acebo Davis, copyright © 1988. It is reproduced with the permission of the artist.

Library of Congress Cataloging-in-Publication Data

Agtuca, Jacqueline R.
    A Community Secret : For the Filipina in an Abusive
Relationship / Jacqueline R. Agtuca
        p.   cm. — (New Leaf series)
    Originally published : [San Francisco] : Asian Women's Shelter,
1992.
    ISBN 1-878067-44-3 : $5.95
    1. Abused wives—California—San Francisco—Case studies.
2. Wife abuse—California—San Francisco—Case studies. 3. Filipinos—Crimes against—California—San Francisco—Case studies.
4. Abused wives—Services for—California—San Francisco. I. Title.
HV6626.22.S4A35   1994   93-23666
362.82'92'08999210794461—dc20   CIP

First published by the Asian Women's Shelter, 1992
First revised Seal Press edition, April 1994
10 9 8 7 6 5 4 3 2 1

Distributed to the trade by Publishers Group West

Acknowledgements

This project is the culmination of the efforts of many women in our community, both immigrant and U.S. born Filipinas. Particular thanks: Christina V. Bernardino; Amihan David; Melissa Cruz; Grace Figueroa; Josefina Figueroa; Ryan Figueroa; Grace Panares; Maria Cecilia Paran; Nerissa Canonizado; Vicky Villena; Amado David; Marlene Marin; Valerie Sheehas; Belsida Ocampo; Irma Chingcuangco; Deania Del Rosario; and Antonia Bello.

The assistance of the Asian American Studies Department at San Francisco State; Family Violence Prevention Fund and Patrick Letellier is also deeply appreciated.

Special recognition is given to the members of the Filipina Advisory Committee of the Asian Women's Shelter who provided leadership and support on this project and so many others.

A special thanks goes to Amihan and Amado David for their continuous support of this project.

This publication is also the result of the dedication and commitment of the staff of the Asian Women's Shelter to providing services to our sisters seeking peace in their homes.

Photographs taken by Susan Breall, pages 11, 20 (top left, top right, lower left), 32; June Miyamoto and Connie Siu, pages 4, 12, 19, 20 (lower right), 26, 40, 60; and Tu-Minh Trinh, page 64.

Project coordination by Cristy Chung and Mimi Kim.

This book is dedicated to
the courageous Filipinas
who have ended
domestic violence in their lives

CONTENTS

Introduction 1

Chapter 1
Katrina's Story 5

Chapter 2
Nene's Story 13

Chapter 3
You Are Not Alone 21

Chapter 4
Ang Mga Anak, The Children 31

Chapter 5
Magdalena's Story 37

Chapter 6
Why Does He Hit Me? 41

Chapter 7
Domestic Violence Kills 47

Chapter 8
The Law Can Help Protect You 53

Chapter 9
We Can End Domestic Violence 61

Chapter 10
Who to Call for Help
Battered Women's Shelters and Hotlines 65

Footnotes 68

Introduction

As a child did you dream that you would grow up, meet that special person and live happily ever after? Katrina, Nene and Magdalena did. But they grew up, got married and became battered women. This book is about their lives and the terrible abuse they and many Filipinas live with every day.

Every word has one goal, to help Filipinas being abused understand they are not alone and that many people in the Filipino community are willing to help them protect themselves.

The fact that only Filipinas are discussed does not mean that Filipino men beat their wives any more than other men, or that the danger is any greater, or that this problem occurs more often in our community than in other communities. We talk about Filipinas because this book is written for every Filipina in a violent relationship and for the Filipino community.

While only the violence by a husband or boyfriend against his wife or girlfriend is discussed, Filipino lesbian and gay men are also battered by abusive partners. It is important that we not tolerate domestic violence in any relationship. Resources for gays and lesbians are included in the back of the book.[1]

The Filipino community can help the women and children being abused by understanding the problem and creating the support and services a Filipina needs to leave her abuser. As a community we can say, "*Kababayan,* leave him. You have a right to live a life free of violence."

Fear, shame, family loyalty or the thought of someone we love being in jail should not stop us from dealing with this problem. The lives of women and children are at risk. Katrina, Nene and Magdalena are three wonderful, intelligent and loving Filipinas. Each married her husband because she fell in love and wanted to spend the rest of her life with him.

Did Katrina ever have the faintest idea that her future husband would someday hold a gun to her head and threaten to pull the trigger? Did Nene ever think the man she married would give her a black eye? Did Magdalena foresee that after her marriage she would be terrorized in her own home? The answer is no, none of these women knew the wonderful person they married was a batterer.

Katrina, Nene and Magdalena met at the Asian Women's Shelter and became very close friends. They are part of a growing family of Filipino women that are ending domestic violence in their lives and homes. Their stories are special yet typical of the experiences of hundreds of Filipinas.

They are courageous women who share their stories in the hope that you can learn to understand that every woman has the right to live free of violence from an abusive relationship — that no man, no husband, no boyfriend has the right to hit a woman. Marriage is not a license to hit. A relationship is not a justification for abuse.

Katrina knows that she will never again have to pick up a chair thrown at her, explain a hole in the wall, or sweep up pieces of a gift from her mother destroyed only to hurt her. Nene no longer fears going home after work. And Magdalena sleeps peacefully knowing she and her children are safe.

Katrina, Nene and Magdalena have ended the domestic violence in their lives, but many of our sisters continue to be abused. Please read their stories and help stop the abuse.

Chapter One
Katrina's Story

Ang Kababayan,

Today is a very special day for me. It is special because I feel strong enough to share my experience with you. I hope my story will help the women that are suffering only because they are involved with a man who believes he has a right to control his wife or girlfriend.

Any woman could become a battered women. It happened to me. It could happen to you, to your grandmother, mother, aunt, sister, daughter, granddaughter or any woman you care about.

I come from a very close and loving family. I am the eldest child and have four wonderful sisters and brothers. My parents worked hard to give us the college education they never had. I was working on my masters in Educational Psychology

His "Forgive me, I won't ever do it again" was said over and over and over. But the abuse continued.

when I left the Philippines. I was active in the church and worked with the disabled and elderly. Life was wonderful, and I was surrounded by people whom I loved. I was happy, but I wanted more independence and thought I could find that independence in America.

The thought that I would become a battered woman never entered my mind.

In the summer of 1988, I met a man who was intelligent, caring and had a great sense of humor. He was a gentleman and a deacon. We became very good friends.

He told me that he attended UC Berkeley Law School and then a management training program at Stanford. This thoughtful and understanding man became my husband one year later. I thought it was a marriage made in heaven. We prayed together and went to church together. I couldn't have asked for more.

Five months later that man disappeared. The man I married became suspicious, accused me of seeing other men, of putting poison in his food, and of stealing his money. He constantly told me that I did things that made him violent. He began to call me names and say things that I had never heard before.

At times he would be furious and then he would say he was sorry, become super nice, buy me gifts, flowers, and chocolates. He would take me to Half Moon Bay, Santa Cruz and Reno as a way of making-up for hitting me. He also took me to expensive restaurants. One day, after an argument, we were waiting for a table and he accused me of making eye contact with a man standing across from us. We immediately left the restaurant.

On the way home he said, "You really don't love me. You just married me to get a green card." I was shocked and started packing my things as soon as we got home. He saw me, knelt down and cried like a little boy. His exact words were, "Don't do this to me. You know how much I love you. I can't stand the thought of another man looking at you. I trust you, but I don't trust them."

He promised never to act that way again and asked me to be patient with him. His "Forgive me, I won't ever do it again" was said over and over and over. But the abuse continued.

He hit me, held a knife to my throat, a gun to my head, and choked me with a golf club. My arms, legs, and body were often covered with bruises. He would kiss them, cry and say, "Baby, I didn't mean to hit you. I don't know why I did it. I lost my temper."

At the time, I couldn't tell anyone what was happening to me. I prayed and hoped that he would change. I asked myself so many whys:

> Why is this happening to me?
> Why is he acting this way?
> Why, God, do you never answer my prayers?

I asked myself if it was fate, chance, or circumstances.

He never let me have money of my own. He wanted to have control over everything I did — even the books I read. He wanted to destroy everything that was important to me. He knew I was proud of being Filipino and would always say, "You're not acting like a good Filipino wife... You just married me for a green card."

I thought that by showing him how much I loved him, how much I cared for him, that he would love me the way I loved him. The more I gave, the more he wanted. I forgot about what I wanted, what I needed. To all of you who think that you can change your husband's violent behavior, you're wrong. I know now that my ex-husband has a serious problem and needs professional help.

His response to my request for us to see a marriage counselor was, "We don't need a stranger in our life." I finally asked him what he wanted me to do so that we would have peace in our home. He said, "Quit your job." He was jealous of the husbands of the women I worked for. In the hope of saving my marriage, I quit work. It was a wonderful time, but it lasted for a very short period.

I told him many times that if he did not change I was leaving. I started packing my belongings to leave many times. But the day I ran out of my home I knew I was running for my life. I knew I could die if I stayed.

I left the night he brutally beat me for answering the telephone. I sat and cried for hours. He left the house and returned drunk and started hitting me again. I grabbed my purse and ran. I had fifteen dollars and the clothes and house slippers I wore. I didn't know where I was going. I was terrorized and ran to the neighbors.

They were shocked when they saw me and called the police. I was covered with bruises, and my nose was swelling. They had been my husband's neighbor for twelve years and thought he was a wonderful man.

> *He knew what he was doing all the time we were married.*

Four police cars arrived. The officers listened to my story and seeing my injuries, were very understanding. One of the officers told me, "A man is not allowed to hit his wife in this country. Many people can help you. This doesn't happen to you alone." He gave me a piece of paper that had the numbers of groups that I could call. The officers treated me well. My only complaint is that different officers, at different times, kept asking me if I was a mail order bride.

My husband was arrested.

I stayed with the neighbors for two nights because the shelters were full. When I went to the shelter I didn't know what to expect, but I had nowhere else to go. I had no family or friends I could stay with. I attended support group meetings and, after hearing the stories of other women in the group, I realized that I was not alone. Some women staying at the shelter had survived worse situations than mine. I met many wonderful people at the shelter at a time when my life was very grim.

The shelters helped me in so many ways besides being a place I could call home. They helped me contact legal assistance which represented me in my dissolution and restraining order hearing, and many other referrals. Most of all, they helped me rebuild my trust in people.

When I was with my husband, I believed that he was violent because he lost his temper. Now I know that he knew what he was doing. He would hit me in places no one could see, places covered by my clothing. He reported my ATM card missing without telling me so that if I left I could not get cash. When my husband married me, he continually talked about my becoming a citizen. He told me he had hired a lawyer, that my application for citizenship was taken care of and not to worry about my immigration status. Today my immigration status is expired and a mess. He knew what he was doing all the time we were married.

My husband was sentenced to twenty (20) days in county jail, two (2) years probation, a fine, and counseling. I feel that justice prevailed although twenty days is too short a time for all the things he did to me.

He robbed me of everything — my love, my trust, my respect, even my thoughts.

The court ordered him to return all of my personal belongings. But everything that I owned and left at our home is missing. There are things of sentimental value that can never be replaced, like the veil my mother gave me on my first communion.

Sometimes I regret leaving what I know was a very good life in the Philippines. But I also know that today I am a different person than I was three years ago. I am more mature, more independent, and have a deeper appreciation for life. I came here because I wanted to be more independent, and the most important thing that I learned in the last three years is that I control my own life.

I hope that those of you who read my story will help women protect themselves from their batterer. A woman can decide to leave and actually leave her abuser, but she needs your help to stop any further violence. To be in an abusive relationship is horrible; it's like living hell. Yes, lots of women stay, and lots go back. But many would leave and not return if they knew they would receive the support I did.

I wish my ex-husband was just a pencil mark in my life so that I could easily erase him from my mind. But he is not.

Today, I have a new job, an apartment and I was selected to participate in a women's self-employment program — the goal of which is to train participants to start their own businesses. But I still live in fear.

I want to thank all of you for taking the time to read my story. Your caring and concern can make a difference. It can save lives. I pray and hope that we can do something to end domestic violence.

God Bless...

Katrina

Chapter Two
Nene's Story

A month after graduation from college with a commerce degree, I eloped with my husband. Life together was so happy and carefree.

He had been previously married, had three children, but was legally separated. In the Philippines divorce is illegal, and someone that is separated can not remarry. But the important thing to us was our love.

The next year I gave birth to our daughter Becka. Rene supported us by driving a taxi. With a new baby I set aside my dream of having a career in advertising. While poor and struggling to make ends meet, we were happy.

When Becka was almost two, Rene received a letter from the United States embassy saying he was an American citizen. The letter said that if he wanted to retain his citizenship he had to reside in the U.S. He left for San Francisco.

I was left in the Philippines, on my own, penniless, homeless and with a daughter to support. I went back to my mother who, although she disapproved of my eloping, was happy to see me and her new grandchild.

Letters, phone calls and money would come from Rene every week. But everything stopped in six months. My letters went unanswered; his phone was disconnected; and I didn't know where he was.

To support myself and Becka, I found a job with a big publishing company as an editorial assistant. I continued writing to Rene, hoping that he would answer my letters. Four years of waiting and praying paid off. He finally called me and said he was coming back for a vacation.

He returned on vacation and said that he forgot about his responsibilities because of women, alcohol, and drugs in San Francisco. He said that he wasn't strong enough to resist them but that he had given that all up now because he knew he wouldn't be happy without us in his life. It didn't matter what had happened in the past as long as he was back.

Rene filed a petition for us, and when Becka was seven, we came to San Francisco. We got married here two weeks after I arrived. I found a job one month later.

From the very beginning of our marriage Rene was very jealous. I pointed out to him that he had no reason to be jealous — that I had remained faithful to him for five years, hoping and waiting, not knowing if he was coming back to me.

He dragged me to an empty Catholic Church one time, and I vowed in front of the altar that I was never unfaithful to him. I thought that my vow would change everything, but it didn't.

I gave birth to my second daughter, Cherry, and we arranged our schedules to take care of the children. He worked during the day, and I worked a swing shift and weekends.

He became more and more jealous. He accused me of flirting with men at work. When I was home, he would call me from his job, and if I didn't answer in two rings, I would have to explain where I was. He would come home unexpectedly, saying he didn't feel well, but I knew he was checking up on me. If I had to do some grocery shopping, I must call him at work before leaving the house and as soon as I got back. I thought, "Well if that's the way you want it, then let it be," just so there would be no arguments or fights.

A year later we were financially doing better and he petitioned for his three children from his former marriage. The children arrived and lived with us. I got a better job and helped support our family as well as his other children. We bought a house in Daly City. I worked the night shift, swing and graveyard.

I would prepare his bath, get his clothes ready for work, make his breakfast and his lunch to take to work. On top of this, I looked after the baby and cooked lunch for the kids. Sometimes I was so tired. But if I didn't do everything, he would accuse me of neglecting him and my responsibilities.

I discovered he still had a girlfriend, plus a son with her. He drank and smoked marijuana. Yet he accused me of being irresponsible and having affairs. In 1989, he was injured on his job and had to stay home. To compensate, I worked overtime to make more money.

Rene became more insecure. If I used the phone, he would accuse me of giving my supposed lover a signal that everything was clear to come into the house. Whenever we were in the car together, if I turned my head sideways, he would slap me and accuse me of looking for my lover's car or for a new man. He called me names like "whore", "flirt", "pig".

Rene hit me across my face, on my neck, and arms. I went to work with bruises, cracked lips and an aching body. He humiliated me. One time he threatened to kill me. He put a knife to my neck while I was holding my baby Cherry. She was only a toddler but still remembers it today.

I tried to defend myself, but he was stronger. I tried to talk him into going to a marriage counselor, but he said that counselors couldn't do anything but pry into our private lives. He dragged me to an empty Catholic Church one time, and I vowed in front of the altar that I was never unfaithful to him. I thought that my vow would change everything, but it didn't.

I tried to run away twice, but both times my husband convinced me he was sorry and that he wouldn't do it again. I went back and secretly hoped that he would change, that he would realize he was wrong and that everything would be right again. But he continued to drink, use drugs and become more violent. Each time he started I became terrified because I knew I would end up getting beaten.

We sold our house with the idea of moving back to the Philippines. We wanted to start a new life. We decided that I would go back with Becka and Cherry, and that he would follow after the house was sold.

A month after I was back in the Philippines, I received a summons from court telling me that I was being sued for divorce and that if I did not respond in 30 days I would lose all claims to the property. I barely had enough money for a plane ticket. I left my children with my family and returned to the States to straighten out matters.

My supervisors were able to reinstate me in my former job. A community law office took my case and helped me file a response to the divorce. Within a month I brought the children back to San Francisco.

My husband withdrew the divorce and persuaded me to go back to him. I believe I was afraid of leaving my husband and loved him so much that I didn't care if the relationship was hurting me.

He promised he would change and we went back to the Philippines once again. We rented an apartment in Manila. Four days later my husband vanished. He took all the money, our green cards and passports.

What opened my eyes to his deception and helped me decide it was over was realizing that he abandoned us. He left us with no money and homeless. If he could do that, he was not worth loving. I decided to fight back.

I sold everything I owned and borrowed money from my family. I went to the U.S. embassy and applied for a temporary travel permit and new passports. I flew with my children to San Francisco.

We moved into a shelter and this time served my husband with divorce papers. At the shelter, everyone was supportive and helpful. On top of food, clothing, and a place to live, they were always there whenever I needed help — a shoulder to lean on, ears to listen, tissue paper always ready to wipe the tears, and words to boost my spirit just when I was running out of it.

While I worked, the volunteers and staff helped with my children. The shelter helped me find permanent housing, a child care center for Cherry, and much more.

I was excited to move to my own apartment, but I didn't know if I could make it. It helped to know that people at the shelter were just a phone call away. They became our extended family in America.

The girls and I stayed in therapy after we left the shelter, and I can say that all of us are better people now. Things are a struggle financially and emotionally. The pain of the separation and losing my husband is still here. I guess it will never heal.

My husband's daughter moved in with me. Now I am supporting three girls, yet the situation gets better every day. I was able to rent an apartment and have furnished it piece by piece — now our little two bedroom apartment looks like a real home.

My youngest will be in kindergarten in September. My oldest daughter is on the honor roll. She wants to be a lawyer and help battered women just like me.

I hope that my story will help you understand what it is like to become a battered woman.

Please do whatever you can to stop domestic violence.

Salamat,

Nene

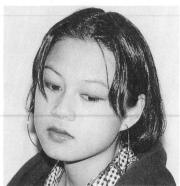

Chapter Three
You Are Not Alone

Madalas na kina-aawaan...,
Madalang maunawaan...

Often pitied...,
Seldom understood...

Katrina tells us how her husband held a knife to her
throat and a gun to her head. Nene speaks about going to
work bruised and with cracked lips.

Why did each of these women stay with her abuser?

Each stayed until she could live with her decision to end
the relationship. "Just leave him," is easy to say, but
every Filipina living with a batterer knows a woman
does not leave until she is ready. Every Filipina living
with a batterer knows that people who say, "Just leave,"
have no idea how difficult, painful and frightening it is to
leave someone that you love even when he believes he
has the right to hit, punch, kick and abuse you.

Katrina and Nene left, but many Filipinas remain involved with a batterer. Intelligent, creative and loving
women stay in an abusive relationship for all kinds of
reasons.

As a Filipina, your batterer's abuse challenges your
identity as a woman, a wife, a mother, or girlfriend. It
places you in a position of fear, loneliness, and insecurity.
His abuse forces you to make decisions that you were
never prepared to make growing up and now must make
away from home without the support of your family.

21

You are not alone. Other Filipinas who were involved with abusive men ended the relationship and were able to make the changes to build a new life.

Violent relationships are dangerous and life-threatening. Sixty-six percent (66%) of the women who were killed in San Francisco in 1990 died because of domestic violence.[1] Domestic violence only gets worse, not better. The violent attacks increase, not decrease.

Although every relationship is different, the following experiences are those of Filipinas who have ended a violent relationship and are now living free of the violence of their batterer. As you read about these experiences, remember that we are each unique, distinct individuals. We come from different islands, speak different dialects, and have had different opportunities. Our reactions to the same situation could be similar or very different from someone else.

I will kill you and your family

"He held my head back, put the gun in my mouth, pulled the hammer back and said, 'If you ever leave me I will kill you.'"

"I was hit so many times, so many different places and ways. During any one of those beatings I could have died. I was afraid to leave, but I knew if I stayed I could die that night, or the next day in my own home. If I stayed he could kill me, but if I left I had the chance of stopping him from hurting me one more time."

"When I was back home, I left him and went to my parents. He came after me, broke down their door and said, 'If you don't come back, I will kill them.' I went back."

"My family is very precious to me. I love them and want to keep them safe and protect them. He threatened to kill them to make me stay with him. As long as it worked, as long I stayed, he continued his threats. Leaving was dangerous, but I knew that they were not safe until he was out of my life. If I stayed any longer, I knew he would do it. The only hope was if I left and was out of his reach, the goal of making me stay would be gone."

"He wanted me to stop seeing my family because he knew they would not allow him to hit me. I stayed away from them for a long time, and that was a mistake. I needed them more than any other time in my life. I needed my family just to know I was still the same person. Stay close to your family. They will help you if they can and if you let them help."

I thought it was me

"He said I looked cheap with mascara on so I stopped wearing mascara. He said I still looked cheap with eye shadow. I stopped wearing eye shadow. I wore no make up, and he said I looked plain. I did everything he wanted, and he still hit me."

"When I was hit, I asked myself, 'What did I do wrong?' I was hit again and again and asked myself again and again, 'What am I doing wrong? How can I change?'"

> *"He said to me every day,*
> *a thousand different ways,*
> *'You made me do it,'*
> *but the truth is, whether*
> *I was an angel or a devil,*
> *he was still a batterer."*

"He was my only family member, friend, the only person that I knew in this country. Instead of looking at his violence, I blamed myself. I quit my job, stopped attending mass, stopped talking to any other man. Over time I changed how I behaved, dressed, and even thought. I felt sad and knew I was losing my self esteem, my confidence, my pride. How could I respect myself if the most important person in my life treated me worse than a stranger?"

"He said to me every day, a thousand different ways, 'You made me do it,' but the truth is, whether I was an angel or a devil, he was still a batterer."

"As a Filipina I was raised to take responsibility for my family, but I know although I married him he is not part of my family. A family respects each other, loves each other, sacrifices for each other. He never respected me, loved me, or sacrificed for me. Whatever he did, he did for himself, not me. I kept his house clean, had sex with him, cooked his food, and as a wife made him a man."

"He said he loved me. I thought he loved me, but who he loved was not me and what he called love was not what I wanted."

"*Mare*, you are not responsible for the home and well being of someone who may kill you."

Nakaka hiya
I am so ashamed

"My family still sends him birthday cards and presents at Christmas. At some point I will tell them he died so that they will stop. I can't tell them he abused me. They would somehow think it was their fault."

"As a little girl I grew up learning that I was responsible for so many things. My success was a tribute to the goodness and wisdom of my parents, and my wrong doings were an embarrassment to not just me but my entire family. Often my mother knew of an argument at school or insult shouted out in anger before I walked in the doorway. Education and employment were important, but even as a little girl I knew marriage was the true indicator of success."

"Most of my family was born, lived, and died in the same barrio. My parents prepared me for many things in life, but they did not prepare me for ending my marriage. I did not even think of leaving, myself, until I had to. How can I explain it to my mother? How do I cope with the humiliation of my parents? How do I tell them it was not their fault — it was not my fault? They would believe me, but they would believe they were somehow responsible, that they did something at some time to cause this to happen to their daughter."

"Growing up, I never knew anyone who got divorced. People got married and stayed married for life. It wasn't just that divorce was illegal. It was not an option in life. I am the first *divorciada* in the history of my family."

"I broke a tradition when I left him, and broke an even greater tradition when I got divorced. But tradition does not justify him beating me. I was forced to leave. I was forced to make the decision to become a *divorciada*. I have nothing to be ashamed of. The shame is his shame, not mine."

I will be deported

"I love my family. My immigration is their future. They survive on the money I send home."

"I came despite all the stories of humiliating working conditions, abuse and even rape. I have seen Filipinas who were doctors take jobs as aides, college graduates take jobs as domestic servants, and I know of many Filipinas who were abused and endured the pain."

"I came just like the 500,000 other Filipino overseas workers because I, like them, do not want to live in poverty. I want to know my family has a future, that my children will be able to go to school and be able to find jobs."

"I stayed because I did not know that the immigration law had changed. A woman married to her petitioner can waive the two year waiting period if she is being abused."

If I leave, I will be all alone here

"Growing up, we were very poor. We played with cans, ants, beetles and each other. We slept on mats on the floor together. Everyone shared almost everything. The houses of my aunties, uncles and cousins were so close we could talk to each other through the window."

"Home was always a place where, despite lots of problems, there was someone to make you feel safe. I have always been surrounded by family. I can't imagine living alone, going home and no one being there."

"Just as important as the *adobo, pan cit,* or *dunuguan* on the table was the family seated around the table. The idea of being alone is as foreign and strange as this country."

"I missed them so much when I came here. I had no one but him. The thought of leaving the only family I had was so scary. Now I have no one but myself. Going home to an empty house is so strange. I have never lived like this. I feel so little and lonely. But I have no other choice."

I can't understand the police

"The police officers could not understand what I was saying. He told them I was screaming because I fell down the stairs and that he was trying to calm me down. I couldn't talk . All I could do was cry. I tried to answer, but they didn't understand me."

"I grew up speaking *Ilocano.* I never learned but a few words of *Tagalog.* I learned English after coming to San Francisco. I can understand what people are saying as long as they don't talk too fast, but because of my accent people sometimes don't understand what I am saying. That was how it was with the police. I also didn't understand them because I was so scared."

"I didn't know about 911. I had no idea that he was committing a crime. I had no idea that I should call the police for help. In my town, an uncle or grandparent would stop something like this — not the police."

"My neighbor got tired of the noise and called the police for me. She finally told me that the police would help me and gave me telephone numbers to call for help. I owe her so much. She helped me when I had no one else. I will always be grateful to her."

No reason is good enough to stay

All of these reasons and many more kept Filipinas from leaving an abusive husband or boyfriend. Each one stayed until she realized no reason was good enough to stay with a batterer and that to protect herself, she could not stay another day. Making the decision to leave does not happen overnight. One Filipina may know she is going to leave after the first incident, but for many others it may take years. On average a woman is attacked six to seven times before she calls the police for help.

All the questions are hard, and many go unanswered. The most important questions that you must ask yourself are:

> *Can I live like this for the rest of my life?*
> *Do I want to grow old being battered?*
> *Do I want my children to grow up seeing me be beaten?*

Talking about or thinking about leaving is much easier than the reality of walking out the door. It is frightening. There are people who can help you — who will understand your fear — who will know the danger you face.

Ang Bayan,

My husband abused me for years and I stayed for many different reasons. One of the most important reasons why I stayed was my children — a daughter and a son.

He told me I could leave but the children had to stay with him and that I would never see them again. At other times he threatened that if I left he would kill both me and the children. I couldn't leave without them and if I took them with me he might come looking for us with his gun.

My son, Rene, wet the bed when he was younger and during the night I would wake up and take him to the bathroom. One day my husband decided that Rene was old enough and told me to stop taking him to the bathroom. The next morning Rene woke up and started crying because he was ashamed and frightened. My husband beat him for wetting the bed. Rene wet the bed until after I left my husband.

I watched Rene grow to fear his father. One day he was playing at a neighbors' and his father called for him but he didn't come. I knew that he couldn't hear his father and ran out the back to get him. Rene knew what was going to happen when he got home and looked at me and said, "Mom, I didn't hear Dad calling me. You know if I did I would have come right away." My son was afraid and I knew I could not protect him.

My children are good kids; they get very good grades and love me. I stayed with my husband because I was afraid of what he might do to them, and finally left because he was treating them the way he treated me. Growing up in a house with a batterer is like living in a war zone. You can be attacked at any time and there is nothing a child can do to fight back. Children need to feel safe in their home but that is not possible when a child lives with a batterer.

We must make our homes safe for our children.

Maraming Salamat,

Aquanita

Chapter Four
Ang Mga Anak
The Children

Imagine hearing your mother scream for help or watching her be beaten. Would you feel angry? Would you be frightened? Now imagine the same experience but as a five year old child living in the same household as a batterer. Domestic violence is a difficult and traumatic experience that can create a living nightmare for a child.

Children living in homes terrorized by a perpetrator of domestic violence have suffered from sleeping disorders, depression, withdrawal, aggressive acting out, finger biting and school problems.[1] Whether the child sees the violent incident or hears the violence the child knows that something is wrong. The violence may confuse and traumatize the child. Studies indicate that children who hear or see incidents of domestic violence are effected the same way as children who are physically and sexually abused.[2] These children live in constant fear of being physically attacked or the fear that another family member will be hit, kicked or beaten.

> *Unless the abuser's behavior is clearly explained, a child can easily believe these excuses and feel responsible for the violence.*

Living with domestic violence can be devastating for a child. It can affect the child for his or her entire life. The negative impact of domestic violence is not only immediate but can affect the child's ability to develop into a well balanced confident adult.

A child has no power over a parent, no authority to make the abuser stop his violence. A child cannot just move out and often has no choice but to continue living with the violence.

Parents are a child's first teachers. Watching an abusive parent sends conflicting messages from which a child can learn that:

- hitting solves problems
- abuse is normal
- fear can make a person do what you want.

A child told not to hit, scream, or call another person names is sent the opposite signal that such behavior is allowed when they watch a batterer's violence.

A child living with a batterer is exposed to abusive behavior and may grow up to be abusive as an adult. Male children in particular may model the behavior of the batterer as an adult. Studies indicate that male children exposed to domestic violence have an increased likelihood of battering their future partners as adults.[3] In other cases children may not wait to become adults to begin to use violence.[4]

I tried to help my mom and my dad kicked me

If your mother was being beaten, would you try to help her? A child will often grab the leg, arm or fist of a batterer in an effort to stop the attack upon his or her mother. As a result a child can be hit, kicked, or struck by weapons intended to injure the child's mother. Children have received injuries such as black eyes, broken bones and abrasions during a batterer's attack. A child may also be intentionally injured or killed by a batterer. In several recent cases Filipino children have been shot by a batterer and in one case the child was killed. Studies indicate that a thirty to forty percent (30-40%) overlap exists in cases of wife beating and child physical or sexual abuse.[5] Shelters for battered women report that the number one reason a woman reports for leaving a batterer is that the batterer was also abusing the children.[6]

Daddy hit Mommy because of me

Domestic violence can cause a child to feel responsible for the abuse. A child can feel guilty and think:

- I didn't stop him
- I called the police and had my father arrested
- My dad hit my mom because I got dirty.

A child may blame his or her self for the batterer's violence. Some of the feelings of guilt may be created by the excuses a batterer may use to justify his violence. A child may hear a batterer say statements such as: "You're not a good mother", "The kids are dirty", or "The kids were bad, why didn't you watch them".

Daddy hit my mom when he came to visit me

Even after the parents of a child are separated a child can continue to feel guilty and responsible for the violence. Children are often used as pawns by a batterer against the mother of his children. Women are often attacked during child visitation — the picking up, return or actual visitation of a child by a batterer is an extremely dangerous time for a woman.

Unless the batterer's behavior is clearly explained a child can easily believe the excuses and feel responsible for the violence. Children may understand that the abuser's behavior is wrong but may need the help of an adult to understand why the abuser is violent. Pretending the violence does not exist, making excuses, or lying to a child is not helpful and may confuse the child and send the message that the violent behavior is acceptable.

Children need to feel safe to grow and develop into healthy adults. A child needs security to feel confident in his or her ability as a human being. Filipino children living in abusive homes need help to stop the violence in their lives. As a community we are compelled to help these children.

1/6

TVIS '90

Chaper Five
Magdalena's Story

Mga Kababayan,

I married my husband because I loved him. He was never violent while we were dating but after our wedding he wanted to know where I went, what I did, and who I talked to. Everyday behavior of going grocery shopping, running errands or visiting with my family became major issues, that often ended in my being hit, beaten and bruised.

He believed our marriage gave him the right to make decisions for me. He thought being married to me gave him the right to control me and abuse me. He didn't see his violence as good or bad — it was just the way a husband acted toward his wife.

He always had an excuse, a reason for his violence. He blamed his violence on something or someone else and never took responsibility for his behavior. Most of the time he blamed me; other times it was something that had happened at work, his drinking or temper. Today I know he abused me because he was a batterer. Hitting me was a choice he made, a decision he made and forced on me.

I remember the day I left my house to help my younger brother. When I returned home my husband was waiting for me and started screaming the moment I walked in the door. He beat me badly all over my body. My mother knocked on our door soon after. She told me later that she had a bad feeling that something had happened to me. He screamed at my mother that he was returning me to her. My mother yelled back, "I welcome my daughter back with open arms."

I was so happy that I could leave him. Looking back, I realize that he had such control over me that he even decided when I could leave. I could leave him because he was making the decision to return me. I was his wife, my children were his children, and he believed this gave him the right to do whatever he wanted to us. In his eyes, whether I lived with him or with my family I still belonged to him.

Domestic violence happens everywhere. It happened to me in the Philippines and it happened to me here in the United States. In the Philippines my husband's abuse was horrible. When it came time for us to move to the United States I didn't want to come. In the Philippines at least I had my family but in the States I would be alone. But my friends told me that in the States it was a crime to beat your wife.

The law may be different in this country but the attitude is the same. No one told me to leave him. His family saw him beat me and never said take the children and leave, you're not safe with him. Neighbors heard me screaming and heard him throwing things at me, but no one called the police.

The last time I left him, he found us and forced the children into his car. He took them to his parents' home and did not allow me to visit. His parents knew he abused me and the children but still blamed me. They were angry because I had left him. My counselor at the shelter said she could help me get them back but I couldn't take the chance so I went back to him.

During my stay at the shelter I met many women. Their stories sounded like my life. No matter what their race or where they came from we shared two things in common: the man that each of us left believed he had the right as a husband to control and beat his wife, and get away with it, and every woman hoped that her batterer would change and she could live in peace.

In the Philippines my husband held me over the edge of a third floor balcony and threatened to drop me. People from below watched but the police never came and no one helped me. In this country after my divorce, my mother, father and I almost died because of his violence. The three of us were hospitalized for days in serious condition.

I now own a business, my divorce is over, I have custody of my children, and my parents and I have recovered from our injuries. If I had understood domestic violence when I married my ex-husband I would have left him and saved myself and my family from the pain his violence caused.

A batterer is a dangerous person. He may be your best friend, son, brother, or father but to the woman he is abusing he is a batterer who is a constant threat and danger. Once a woman is abused she knows it can happen again, any place or any time. Don't make excuses for his abuse; tell him he has to take responsibility for his violence.

I hope that my story helps the Filipino community understand that a woman has a right to live free of violence. Filipino women and children will continue to suffer and die until we as a community believe that domestic violence is never acceptable.

Salamat,

Magdalena

Chapter Six
Why Does He Hit Me?

Do you think to yourself, "I'm tired. I had a horrible day. But I don't hit him?" Do you ever think, "He hits me because he's drunk," or "He hits me because he can't control his temper?" The answer to the question "Why does he hit me?" is very simple. He hits you because he chooses to hit you. He chooses to be a batterer. He will continue to be a batterer until he chooses to stop being a batterer. Why any man makes the choice to be a batterer is a more difficult question to answer. Here are some of the reasons that we believe men batter.

Any man could be a batterer

Abusive behavior has nothing to do with age, profession, family background or education. A batterer might be Mr. Wonderful to everyone except his wife or girlfriend. Because a batterer treats other people well does not mean that he treats his wife or girlfriend well.

"I didn't mean to do it," are words that describe an accident. A batterer's violence is no accident.

Being a wonderful son, brother or neighbor does not excuse a man's violence toward his wife or girlfriend. An abuser is defined by his use of violence and not our relationship to him. If he abuses his wife or girlfriend, he is a batterer.

I didn't mean to hit her, I just lost my temper

An abuser knows that his violence is wrong and may never think of punching someone in the face because he disagrees with what they said or did. A batterer may use the excuse, "It was an accident. I just lost my temper." But he controls his temper going to work, while at work, and with other people. The fact that he loses it with his wife means he believes that he can hit her and nothing will happen to him. His violence is the problem. His temper is an excuse.

A batterer will often justify his violence and blame someone else for his abusive behavior. Excuses a batterer has used to justify his violence include:

- You are not a good Filipino wife
- You are getting too Americanized
- *Bastos ka* or you are disrespectful
- You are unfaithful.

None of these reasons can justify a batterer's abuse. Hitting a woman because you don't like something she said or did is inexcusable and intolerable. A batterer doesn't have to hit. He chooses to hit.

I make the decisions in my house

Violence gives the abuser control and power. The control may start with the batterer making small unimportant decisions about the relationship and then grow to his making all the decisions about your life. The violence is intended to enforce his control and authority.

Other ways an abuser can control a Filipina are:

- insulting you in front of others
- confiscating your mail from relatives
- not letting you have any money
- telling you what you can or cannot wear.

This type of control is very damaging and creates a relationship in which he makes all the decisions and you make no decisions. This unequal standard can gradually become accepted and considered normal.

Filipinas have described other abusive acts such as: He would get his gun out and clean it if I didn't do exactly what he wanted. He would load it, point it at me and then unload it. He would hold a favorite dish in the air and drop it just to let me know he was the boss. He would cut up a favorite dress. If I got upset he would demand to know who I was trying to look good for.

"I didn't mean to do it," are words that describe an accident. A batterer's violence is no accident. The abuse occurs again and again, often increasing in severity and frequency. Over time, name calling turns into hitting; a slap becomes a fist; and eventually what was once unacceptable begins to happen every day.

Violent behavior is learned

A batterer is not born violent. He learned to be violent. He could have learned his violence as a child by watching his role models or, as an adult, from society.

Some abusers saw their mother abused when they were a child, but others were raised by non-violent parents and learned to be violent from society. Violence against women is a common theme on television, movies and advertisements.

Violence against Filipinas is reinforced by the image of women in our community. The image of a Filipina portrayed in the "Komiks", on the back of the jeepney mud flaps, or the San Miguel Beer and Hope cigarette advertisements all send a message that women are sex objects and men can abuse them.

An abuser must unlearn his violence

An abuser can unlearn his violent behavior if he understands that it is wrong and will not be tolerated in our community.

An abuser must learn that:

- he does not have the right to hit
- he cannot use violence to control the Filipina
- his manhood is not dependent on controlling his wife or girlfriend's life.

Anger is a normal response to a problem. Violence is not. Domestic violence is not romantic. It is not an expression of love. It is abusive behavior that has one goal — to control the person being abused.

I'm sorry, please forgive me

If you hurt someone, you may say, "I'm sorry, please forgive me." These words would mean nothing if after the person forgives the incident, you act the same way and hurt them again. Batterers say, "I'm sorry," again and again.

How many times must a woman be assaulted before it becomes clear that the words "I'm sorry" do not mean "I won't do it again?" Only a batterer can change his behavior. His violence and not the acceptance of his apology is the only issue.

PENANCE   TANS '86

Mga Kababayan,

My sister's death did not begin with her murder — it began years ago when he first called her a whore. It started with the pushing, the hitting and kicking.

She called the police; I called the police; the neighbors called the police. Every time he begged forgiveness, his family pressured her to pity him, and friends told her she would ruin his life by putting him in jail.

He broke her nose, bent her finger back so far it broke and gave her bruises, but everyone always pitied him. Now that he's killed her people still pity him. They still say: We have to help him. . . He's a Filipino. . . He just lost control . . . .

He abused her for five years and knew what he was doing the whole time. She could have died during any one of those beatings. Was her life less important because she was his wife?

I want to ask the community to start worrying about the women and children being abused. Let's work together to end the violence in the homes of our families.

Salamat,

Maria

Chapter Seven
Domestic Violence Kills

The FBI reports that one third of the women killed in this country are killed by a husband or boyfriend.[1] This statistic, while shocking, does not reflect the real number of women that die each year at the hands of a husband or someone they dated. A recent study in San Francisco found that domestic violence is the largest category of solved homicide cases. Fifty-nine percent (59%) of all of the women killed in San Francisco died because of family violence.[2] These statistics tell us that the most dangerous place for a woman is in her own home. The reality that a woman is most likely to be killed, raped or seriously injured by a man she married or dated is a fact that is not widely known by the public.

The Filipino community is no exception to this national epidemic. The murders and attempted murder of Filipinas in San Francisco, Seattle, and Hawaii made headlines this last year.[3]

A domestic violence homicide does not begin with the act of murder; it often begins years earlier. While the trial of a homicide case may make front page news, the type of day-to-day abuse preceding the murder is frequently ignored. Stopping such abuse in these cases is a critical link to preventing these unnecessary deaths.

Many Filipinos think that domestic violence is part of our culture; other Filipinos believe it only happens in other cultures, and still others think it is part of Asian culture. In a number of murder cases in which a Filipino or Asian man stood trial for the murder of his wife, culture was raised as a legal defense to the crime. These cases are controversial and received mixed responses from the community.

In Hawaii, Mr. Ganal, a Filipino man, shot his wife of 19 years, then shot their son in the mouth, and finally killed her parents. Mrs. Ganal had left him and refused his pleas that she return to him. He then burned to the ground the former home of her boyfriend, resulting in the death of a man, a toddler and a 10 month old infant. At his trial his attorney presented an expert witness who testified on the cultural issues of amok and amor propio (self-esteem). Mr. Ganal's defense to the charges of first-degree murder and first-degree attempted murder was in part Filipino culture.[4]

In New York, Dong Lu Chen, a Chinese man, bludgeoned his wife to death with a hammer.[5] He believed that she was having an affair with another man. At his trial an expert witness testified that in Chinese culture, a woman's adultery is proof of her husband's weak character and a source of great shame. Charged with first degree murder, Mr. Chen was allowed to plead guilty to manslaughter and sentenced to five years' probation.[6] According to the judge the defendant was driven to violence by traditional Chinese values about adultery and loss of manhood.

In the San Joaquin Valley of California, a Hmong man from Laos was arrested and charged with rape and kidnapping. The man argued his abduction and rape of the woman was a traditional Hmong marriage ritual, know as zij poj niam.[7] The prosecutor reduced the charges to the misdemeanor of false imprisonment and the judge sentenced the defendant to pay a $1,000 fine and ninety days in county jail.[8]

In each of the above cases an Asian woman was killed or raped by a man of the same culture. Each man claimed at trial his violent attack was due in part to his cultural heritage. This assertion is a dangerous one because while phrased in cultural terms it is in reality a argument that violence against women is acceptable and legal.

The absurdity of such a claim would be laughable if not for the reality that in every case expert witnesses on culture testified on behalf of the defendant. Unfortunately, the criminal justice system in an effort to be culturally sensitive allowed such testimony, and often reduced the charge to a lesser offense and granted a lighter sentence.

Women of every race are killed each year by their husbands, but in these and other recent cases involving Asian men such behavior was viewed as cultural. Murder, rape and physical violence against women by Asian men is no more cultural than it is for European men. Horrible acts of domestic violence are inflicted on women by members of every ethnic group and such arguments by defense attorneys and the acceptance of them by prosecutors and judges only perpetuates a racist stereotype that such behavior is condoned in Filipino and other Asian cultures.

Just as appalling as the acceptance of cultural arguments in domestic violence cases by the criminal justice system is the reality that many people of every race still believe that such behavior is reasonable, if not excusable. Sections of the specific cultural community often pressure the court and the prosecutor to be lenient on the defendant. Obviously culture is not strictly the domain of a man; the woman in each case also had a claim on culture and tradition. Each woman's right to live according to her traditional and cultural values, free of violence is often ignored and her cry for justice unheard.

The long history of a husband's right to physically abuse his wife in this country can be traced back to early Roman and then British Law. A husband's physical abuse of his wife was not considered a crime, and early Roman Law permitted a man to beat his wife to the point of death. In 753 B.C. the Laws of Chastisement were enacted and the first legal restriction on the weapons a husband could use to chastise his wife was established. The law allowed a man to beat his wife as long as the "rod he used was no larger than his thumb." This case is the source of the old expression "rule of thumb."[9]

Clearly, domestic violence was legal until only recently in both Europe and the United States. It cannot be isolated to a social practice occurring only in Asia and among people of Asian ancestry. Society has a long history of accepting domestic violence between a husband and wife but domestic violence is not cultural. The physical, sexual and mental abuse that constitutes the pattern of behavior called domestic violence is a form of torture and terrorism. Domestic violence, like slavery in the United States, was a legal reality that was socially acceptable. The slaves bought and sold on the auction block never accepted slavery as cultural and women in the past and present do not accept physical abuse as cultural.

Today, every state in this country has enacted legislation that makes domestic violence a crime. While the laws have changed, social attitudes have a long way to go. Police often listen to the abuser, prosecutors often plea bargain the case and judges often accept a recommendation of a lighter sentence. Tragically, community members frequently encourage the court to be lenient toward the man.

In this pool of sympathy toward the abuser, the reality of the living hell the batterer created for his victim is lost. Women have resisted being battered and abused even when the law said the opposite. When will the voices of these women be heard and their culture of resistance to domestic violence be recognized?

Domestic violence is a pattern of behavior and not a single act. Often domestic violence is not recognized or named until the violence results in a serious injury or the police are called; even after an outside party has intervened many choose to excuse the behavior as an unfortunate mistake. Domestic violence is not an unfortunate mistake, it is a pattern of conduct by one person that is imposed upon another.

While many issues need attention in our community, domestic violence must be prioritized. A study of family violence found that all of the Filipinas murdered in San Francisco during 1991 and 1992 were killed by their husband or boyfriend.[10] If these women were murdered by a stranger, or a racist or because they were immigrants the Filipino community would be demanding justice.

Domestic violence is a man-made social ill that is perpetuated and passed from one generation to the next generation. It is possible to end domestic violence in our homes and it is possible that men who are batterers can change. While this change must come from within each abuser, change must also come from within our community. We as a community must say in a unified voice that domestic violence is intolerable. We as a community must join together to change the shocking reality that the most dangerous place for a Filipina is her home.

**One-third of all female homicide victims in this country
are killed by a husband or boyfriend.**
(FBI, *Uniform Crime Reports*, 1988)

**Each year 2.1 million married, separated, or divorced
women in the United States are beaten by their partners.**
(Langan, Patrick; Innes, Christopher, *Bureau of Justice Statistics Special Report*
"Preventing Domestic Violence Against Women,"
Washington, DC: US Department of Justice, August 1986, p.3)

**Studies show that 22% to 35% of women visiting
hospital emergency rooms are there due to symptoms
related to ongoing abuse by a partner.**
(*Journal of the American Medical Association*,
August 22/29, 1990-Vol 264, No. 8, p. 934)

**Battering is the single major cause of injury to women,
even more significant than the numbers injured in
auto accidents, rapes or muggings combined.**
(O'Reilly, Jane, 1983. "Wife Beating: The Silent Crime,"
Time Magazine, September 5)

**Shelters report the number one reason
women give for leaving is that the batterer was
also attacking the children.**
(Survey conducted at New Beginnings Shelter for battered women,
Seattle, Washington, 1990)

**Boys who witness violence between their parents
are almost three times more likely to become batterers
than are sons of nonviolent parents.**
(Straus, M.; Gelles, R.; Steinmetz, S. *Behind Closed Doors: Violence in the
American Family*. Garden City, New York: Anchor Press/Doubleday, 1980. p. 16)

**Forty-four million dollars in medical cost is incurred
each year because of domestic violence.**
(National Crime Surveys: National Sample, 1973-1979.
American Journal of Public Health, 70:65-66, 1989)

Chapter Eight
The Law Can Help Protect You

There are many laws that can help a Filipina protect herself from a violent partner. These laws include prosecuting a batterer in criminal court or filing an action against him in civil court. Before deciding on a legal plan, talk to someone that knows the law.

The criminal system

If the abuse caused injuries such as bruises, cuts, swelling, a pulled muscle, or a fracture, he can be arrested. In California, the state prosecutor can charge an abuser who injures his wife, girlfriend, former girlfriend, or woman with whom he has a child with a crime.

If the injuries are serious, he can be charged with a felony which can result in a sentence of over a year in jail. If the injuries are minor, he can be charged with a misdemeanor which can result in a sentence of less than a year in jail. Serious threats should also be reported to the police.

The judge can also sentence an abuser to attend domestic violence counseling and issue a stay away order, requiring him to stay at least 150 feet away from the Filipina and her home or job, and to not contact her by telephone, mail, or through other people. Abusers can also be sentenced to a period of probation.

What should I do if he is attacking me?

If the batterer is attacking you, call 911 and tell them you are being beaten and need help immediately. Don't hang up. All 911 calls are recorded and can be used as evidence during a trial.

Family Violence is the Leading Motive in Solved Homicide Cases [1]

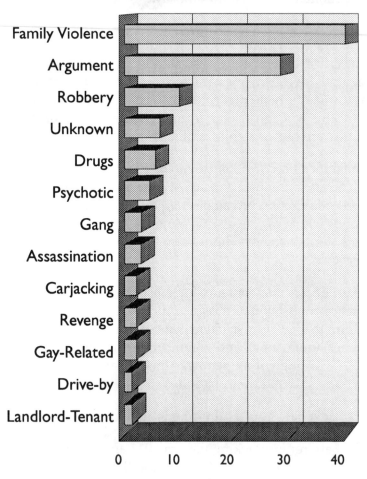

Total = 30 Female Victims in Solved Homicides in 1991-1992

When the police arrive, tell them you want the abuser arrested. If they refuse to make the arrest, tell them you want to make a *citizen's arrest*. Insist that you are given a police incident report number. If you have injuries, ask the police to get you medical assistance. The police should also take photographs of your injuries as evidence of the attack. You should tell the officers about anyone else who may have heard or seen the attack. They can be witnesses in the case.

If you cannot call the police at the time of the attack, call or go to the police station as soon as you can. Save any evidence of the abuse that can be used to show the attack happened.

What should I do after making the report

Remember that calling the police is just the first step. You must follow your case each step of the way. Call your local domestic violence shelter or other support services for help.

Don't be afraid to participate with the Assistant District Attorney. The District Attorney's office is there to prosecute criminal behavior. The prosecutor can help you stop future violent attacks by your batterer. It's their job to prosecute crimes and help protect you, your family and community.

Over Half of All Female Homicide Victims are Victims of Family Violence

59%

Female Victims of Family Violence

41%

Other Female Victims

Total = 30 Female Homicide Victims in 1991-1992

Civil law

The civil court provides other options which include dissolving the marriage, custody of the children, child support, money for injuries from the abuse, and a restraining order. A restraining order, like a stay away order, tells the abuser he must stay 150 feet away from the people listed on the order. It is important to remember that in many states a wife is entitled to one half of all property acquired during the marriage.

Civil court issues are complicated, and it is recommended that you obtain a lawyer to represent you in civil court. Do not sign any court papers without discussing them with a lawyer. Legal assistance programs exist in most areas that can represent women unable to hire a lawyer.

Family Violence is the Leading Cause of Death for Female Victims in Solved Cases

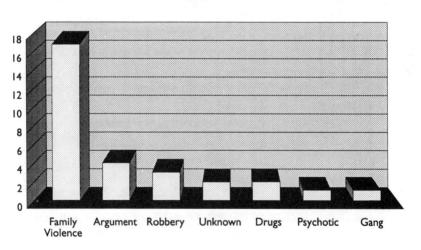

Total = 30 Female Victims in Solved Homicides in 1991-1992

Immigrant Status and the Law[2]

In the United States domestic violence is considered criminal conduct whether the victim is a citizen or not. Police officers, prosecutors and criminal court judges will generally not ask or turn a woman reporting domestic violence into the INS. You also do not need to be a citizen or legal permanent resident to obtain a protective order and civil court judges also do not generally ask about the immigration status of a woman in such cases.

You may get a divorce (dissolution) in the U.S. even if you are not a U.S. citizen, or legal permanent resident, and not married in the U.S. You can get a divorce even if your husband does not agree. If you divorce in the U.S., only U.S. laws will be used by the court. If you are served with divorce or annulment papers you should contact a lawyer immediately. An annulment or divorce could terminate your immigration status.

If you have permanent resident status or are a legal refugee your legal status should not be affected. It is very important that you keep documents and any items that can show your marriage was real and not entered into only for immigration purposes. Items that can show your marriage was real include: a lease or mortgage showing that you share a home a home or apartment, records of joint bank accounts or other financial records, any love letters, photos of you and your husband as a couple, and telephone numbers and addresses of friends who knew you as a couple.

If you are a victim of battery or extreme cruelty and you have conditional residency, you will still be able to keep lawful immigration status. If your husband will not cooperate in removing your conditional status you can ask for a waiver. Contact an immigration attorney or one of the organizations listed in Chapter 10 for information about the Spousal Abuse Waiver to the Marriage Fraud Act.

If the father of your children is threatening to take your children away or take them to his home country you should take the following precautions as soon as possible. Obtain a court order stating you have custody of your children. The order can also prohibit the father of the children from removing the children from the country in which you live. If the children are U.S. citizens, send a copy of this order to the embassy of the father of your children. Also send a copy of the order to the U.S. Department of State (Office of Passport Services, 202/326-6168) to prevent the issuance of passports and visas for the children. A copy of the order should be given to the children's schools and you should tell the school administrators not to release the children to anyone but yourself. Lastly, make sure you have recent photos, passports and birth certificates for the children. Keep a list of addresses and telephone numbers of the father's friends and relatives in his home country.

If you are a U.S. citizen, lawful permanent resident or possess valid visas, you cannot be deported unless you entered the U.S. on fraudulent documents, violated conditions of your visas, or have been convicted of certain crimes.

If you are undocumented or unsure of your immigration status you should seek the assistance of an immigration attorney to see if you can legalize your status. Until then, you should do what you need to make yourself safe.

Chapter Nine
We Can End Domestic Violence

Every day each of us can make a difference in our own way. Domestic violence happens because batterers believe they have the right to be abusive and that no one will stop them.

No child is born wanting to be an abused woman or born wanting to be a batterer. We learn what is acceptable or unacceptable behavior. As a sister, brother, aunt, uncle, parent, friend or neighbor we can say in a thousand ways, "Domestic violence is never acceptable."

We can each say in our own way that no person deserves to be abused; that every woman has the right to live a life free of violence and the threat of violence.

Domestic violence happens everyday in our community. It is a well known secret that must be stopped. Katrina, Nene and Magdalena are not alone. You are not alone. As long as one woman is abused in her home, any woman can be. As long as one woman is abused, every woman is in danger.

If you know someone who is involved with an abuser, you can help:

Name the violence. Ignoring, excusing, or justifying domestic violence does not help. Domestic violence is serious and can be deadly. You can educate others to see the seriousness of domestic violence.

Believe her. If someone you know has the courage to tell you about the violence, believe her immediately.

Do not blame her. It is all too common to question the behavior of the woman and not the batterer. Domestic violence is wrong no matter what.

Help her find other options. Many battered Filipinas stay in abusive situations because they see no alternatives. Their batterers often prevent them from seeking even emotional support. You may talk to her about resources, help her come up with a safe plan, accompany her to services, offer her a place to stay, etc.

Respect her decisions. Ending a relationship with an abusive partner can be very dangerous, and a safe plan for leaving should be created if possible. While we as family, friends or neighbors want to help, the Filipina ending the relationship knows best what will work and not work. She has survived the abuse and understands the dangers that may arise while she is taking the steps towards a life free of violence.

It is time for the Filipino community to recognize that every Filipina has the right to make her own decisions, determine her own future, and control her body. We must raise our daughters to stand on equal ground with their Filipino brothers in intelligence and leadership both in the public and at home.

Please join the thousands of women and men working to stop domestic violence.

Tu-Mihn Trinh is a photographer and Children's Advocate at the Asian Women's Shelter. The two children she has captured in this image stayed at the Shelter. They represent our hope for breaking the cycle of violence.

Chapter Ten
Who to Call for Help
Battered Women's Shelters and Hotlines

Shelters for battered women are safe places women who are abused can go to live for a short time. They are in secret locations so that all women who go there will be safe. They can help you with the legal system and can help you plan your new life. Shelters and crisis lines or hotlines are places you can call so that you can talk to someone who understands what you are going through. They can help you in an emergency. It may be uncomfortable to talk to a stranger about your problems, but many women call the crisis line daily to seek help. Anything you share will be kept strictly confidential.

A Filipina who calls a shelter can talk to a counselor. If you do not speak English, some shelters can have someone that speaks your dialect return your call. A counselor can listen to your concerns and fears, help develop a plan for leaving the abuser if you wish, and make necessary legal referrals to discuss immigration, divorce or how to obtain a protective order.

If you are afraid for your safety or that of your children, you can stay at a shelter. When you are ready to leave a shelter, a counselor can help you develop a plan for the future. Many Filipino women have stayed at shelters and have gone on to live free of domestic violence.

One of the battered women's shelters in San Francisco is the Asian Women's Shelter. It is a special place and a temporary home to many Asian women and children. The Asian Women's Shelter was created by a group of

Asian women who understand the problem of domestic violence in our community. They realize that battered Asian women need services that recognize and are sensitive to our distinct cultures.

The Asian Women's Shelter supports a woman's right to live according to traditional cultural values without having to risk her physical safety and emotional well being.

IF YOU ARE BEING ABUSED...

- Tell someone whom you trust.
- Remember that no one deserves to be beaten.
- You are not alone.
- Call the resources in the next section for assistance, information, and/or shelter.

IF YOU ARE AN ABUSER...

- Seek help.
- If you ignore the problem, it will only get worse.
- Call counseling services for batterers listed in the next section for help.

IF YOU KNOW SOMEONE WHO IS IN A RELATIONSHIP WHERE THERE IS VIOLENCE...

- Urge them to seek help.
- Call the resources in the next section for referral information.

Asian Women's Shelter (San Francisco)
(415) 731-7100

New York Asian Women's Center
(212) 732-5200

Center for Asian Pacific Families (Los Angeles)
(213) 653-4042

Family Violence Prevention Fund (San Francisco)
(415) 821-4553

Immigrant Assistance Line
(415) 554-2444
(English & Spanish)

(415) 554-2454
(Cantonese, Mandarin, Vietnamese)

National Lawyers Guild
National Immigration Project
(617) 227-9727

The National Coalition Against Domestic Violence
(303) 839-1852

Community United Against Violence
Gay and Lesbian Domestic Violence
(415) 777-5500

Footnotes
Introduction

1. Island, D., & Letellier, P., "Men Who Beat the Men Who Love Them" Harrington Park Press, 1991.

Chapter 3

1. Domestic Violence 1990 Homicide Study, conducted by the Family Violence Prevention Fund, San Francisco, California (1991).

Chapter 4

1. Jaffe, P.G., Wolfe, D.A., & Wilson, S.K. "Children of Battered Women" Newbury Park, CA: Sage, 1990.

2. Goodman, G. & Rosenberg, M., "The Child Witness to Family Violence: Clinical and Legal Considerations" In Sonkin, D., ed, Domestic Violence on Trial: Psychological and Legal Dimensions of Family Violence, Springer, 1986.

3. Hotteling, G.T. & Sugarman, D.B., "An Analysis of Risk Markers in Husband to Wife Violence: The Current State of Knowledge" Violence and Victims, 1(2), 101-124, 1986.

4. Ganley, A.L., "The Impact of Domestic Violence on the Defendant and the Victim in the Courtroom" In Domestic Violence: The Crucial Role of the Judge in Criminal Court Cases, A National Model for Judicial Education, Family Violence Prevention Fund, San Francisco, CA, 1991.

5. See note 1.

6. Based on a survey conducted at New Beginnings, a shelter for battered women in Seattle, Washington, 1990, cited in note 4.

Chapter 7

1. U.S. Dept. of Justice, Uniform Crime Reports 1985 (Washington D.C., FBI 1986), p. 11.

2. Domestic Violence 1991 and 1992 Homicide Study, conducted by the Family Violence Prevention Fund, San Francisco, California (1993).

3. There was one murder-suicide in Seattle, Washington; one attempted murder in Honolulu, Hawaii and two murders in San Francisco, California.

4. Honolulu Star-Bulletin, April 7, 1993.

5. People v. Chen, No. - (N.Y. Sup. Ct. 1989).

6. Choi, "Application Of A Cultural Defense In Criminal Defense Proceedings" 8:80 Pacific Basin Law Journal, 1990, p. 80.

7. Sherman, "Cultural" Defense Draw Fire, Nat'l L.J., April. 17, 1989, p. 28.

8. People v. Moua, No. 315972 (Fresno Super. Ct. 1985).

9. Stedman, Beirne, "Right of Husband to Chastise Wife," 3 Va. Law Reg. 241 (1917).

10. Family Violence Prevention Fund 1993 Homicide Study, cited in note 2.

Chapter 8

1. All three charts contained in this chapter were produced by the Family Violence Prevention Fund and the San Francisco Commission on the Status of Women. All statistical information refers to solved

homicide cases in the city of San Francisco during 1991 and 1992. Copies of the study can be obtained from the Commission on the Status of Women, 25 Van Ness, San Francisco, CA, 941101.

2.   Information contained in this section was obtained from a brochure entitled "You Have a Right to be Free from Violence in Your Home, Questions and Answers for Immigrant and Refugee Women", produced by Donna Norton and the Family Violence Prevention Fund in collaboration with the Coalition for Immigrant and Refugee Rights and Services/Immigrant Women's Task Force, Asian Women's Shelter, Asian Law Caucus and the San Francisco Neighborhood Legal Assistance Foundation. The brochure is available in Spanish, Chinese, Tagalog, and Korean. For more in-depth coverage, consult the manual, "Domestic Violence in Immigrant and Refugee Communities: Asserting the Rights of Battered Women". The brochure and manual can be ordered from the Family Violence Prevention Fund, Bldg. 1, Suite 200, 1001 Potrero Avenue, San Francisco, CA, 941101.

Jacqueline R. Agtuca, J.D., is a member of the
Board of Directors of the Asian Women's Shelter
in San Francisco, California. Through her work
at the Family Violence Prevention Fund, she
works with Filipinas who are ending domestic
violence in their lives. Ms. Agtuca also teaches
at the Asian American Studies and Women
Studies Departments of San Francisco State
University.

OTHER TITLES AVAILABLE FROM SEAL PRESS

GETTING FREE: *You Can End Abuse and Take Back Your Life* by Ginny NiCarthy. $12.95, 0-931188-37-7. The most important self-help resource book of the domestic violence movement. 120,000 copies sold! *NOW ON AUDIOCASSETTE:* GETTING FREE: *Are You Abused? (And What to Do About It)* narrated by Ginny NiCarthy (based on the book) 60 minutes. $10.95, 0-931188-84-9.

YOU CAN BE FREE: *An Easy-to-Read Handbook for Abused Women* by Ginny NiCarthy and Sue Davidson. $8.95, 0-931188-68-7. A simplified version of the national bestseller, GETTING FREE.

TALKING IT OUT: *A Guide to Groups for Abused Women* by Ginny NiCarthy, Karen Merriam and Sandra Coffman. $12.95, 0-931188-24-5. An informative and comprehensive handbook for counselors, mental health workers, and shelter or community activists on starting and sustaining a group for abused women.

THE ONES WHO GOT AWAY: *Women Who Left Abusive Partners* by Ginny NiCarthy. $12.95, 0-931188-49-0. This book takes us directly into the lives of more than thirty women who left abusive partners and started their lives over.

YOU DON'T HAVE TO TAKE IT!: *A Woman's Guide to Confronting Emotional Abuse at Work* by Ginny NiCarthy, Naomi Gottlieb and Sandra Coffman. $14.95, 1-878067-35-4. This comprehensive guide provides practical advice and exercises to help women recognize abusive situations and respond with constructive action, including assertive confrontation and workplace organizing.

MEJOR SOLA QUE MAL ACOMPAÑADA: *For the Latina in an Abusive Relationship/Para la Mujer Golpeada* by Myrna Zambrano. $10.95, 0-931188-26-1. A bilingual handbook in Spanish and English offering support, helpful advice, understanding and practical information on many issues and questions about abusive relationships.

CHAIN CHAIN CHANGE: *For Black Women Dealing with Physical and Emotional Abuse* edited by Evelyn C. White. $5.95, 0-931188-25-3. *Chain Chain Change* is for the black woman who wants to understand the role of emotional abuse and violence in her life, and for the activist and professional who works with domestic violence.

DATING VIOLENCE: *Young Women in Danger* edited by Barrie Levy. $16.95, 1-878067-03-6. Both a call for action and a tool of change, this book is the first comprehensive resource for teens in sexually, emotionally or physically abusive relationships.

IN LOVE AND IN DANGER: *A Teen's Guide to Breaking Free of Abusive Relationships* by Barrie Levy. $8.95, 1-878067-26-5. An important, straightforward book for teens caught in abusive dating relationships.

SEAL PRESS, founded in 1976 to provide a forum for women writers and feminist issues, has many other titles in stock: fiction, self-help books, anthologies and international literature. Any of the books above may be ordered from us at 3131 Western Avenue, Suite 410, Seattle, Washington, 98121 (please include 15% of total book order for shipping and handling). Write to us for a free catalog.